DO - IT - YOURSELF

PAINTING
SKILLS

DO-IT-YOURSELF

PAINTING
SKILLS

Mike Lawrence

LORENZ BOOKS

This edition is published by Lorenz Books,
an imprint of Anness Publishing Ltd,
Blaby Road,
Wigston,
Leicestershire LE18 4SE;

info@anness.com

www.lorenzbooks.com;
www.annesspublishing.com

If you like the images in this book and
would like to investigate using them for
publishing, promotions or advertising,
please visit our website
www.practicalpictures.com for more
information.

Publisher: Joanna Lorenz
Editors: Felicity Forster, Anne Hildyard
Photographer: John Freeman
Illustrator: Andrew Green
Designer: Bill Mason
Production Controller: Mai-Ling Collyer

Additional text: Sacha Cohen

ACKNOWLEDGEMENTS AND NOTES
The publisher would like to
thank The Tool Shop for supplying
tools for jacket photography:
97 Lower Marsh
Waterloo, London SE1 7AB
Tel 020 7207 2077; Fax 020 7207 5222
www.thetoolshop-diy.com

The author and publishers have made
every effort to ensure that all instructions
contained within this book are accurate
and safe, and cannot accept liability for
any resulting injury, damage or loss to
persons or property, however it may arise.
If in any doubt as to the correct procedure
to follow for any home improvements
task, seek professional advice.

CONTENTS

INTRODUCTION

Painting walls, woodwork and other surfaces is, so all the surveys reveal, by far the most popular do-it-yourself job.

Modern paints and several improvements in the design and manufacture of decorating tools have certainly made the task less arduous than it was in the days of traditional oil-bound paints and distemper (tempera), and have also made it easier for the amateur decorator to obtain professional-looking results.

One major shift in paint technology is the trend away from using solvent-based varnishes and paints for wood, toward water-based products that do not give off harmful vapours as they dry. Water-based finishes are not as durable as solvent-based ones, but are no longer as far behind them in performance terms as they once were, and they have other advantages, such as faster drying times, virtually no smell and easier cleaning of brushes, rollers and pads. Therefore, it is likely that their use in the home will become much more widespread.

No amount of clever technology can eliminate the need for proper preparation of the surfaces to be decorated, even though this

ABOVE: Traditional household paints are either water-based (latex) or solvent-based (oil) and are generally available in three finishes: matt (flat), satin (mid sheen) and gloss.

ABOVE: Careful preparation is one of the keys to successful painting. Buy a dust sheet (dust cover) and use a sturdy set of steps to reach the tops of walls and ceilings.

part of the job is far less enjoyable and often more time-consuming than the actual painting. In many cases, it involves little more than washing down the surface, but sometimes more thorough preparation will be called for.

This book describes the various types of paint, varnish and stain on the market; which to use where;

how to prepare surfaces for redecoration; how to apply the new finish – especially to the more awkward surfaces, such as windows and panelled doors – and how to create a range of special paint effects that can be used to make dramatic and inexpensive alternatives to traditional wall coverings.

OPPOSITE: Emulsion (latex) paint is available in a huge range of ready-mixed colours. Most basic wall painting is done with water-based emulsion (latex) paint since it is easy to apply with a variety of brushes, rollers, sponges and rags. Several layers can be painted over each other.

RIGHT: Different paints are suitable for different surfaces and effects, so it is very important that you choose the right paint for the right surface.

MATERIALS & EQUIPMENT

There are some basic essentials that you will need for decorating. You can add to this equipment gradually as you work on different effects. For general painting, edging and painting woodwork, use household paintbrushes. The most useful sizes are 50mm (2in) and 25mm (1in). Finer artist's brushes are invaluable for dealing with difficult small spaces and touching up odd areas. Soft sable-haired artists' brushes with rounded edges are best for this purpose. When painting walls and ceilings, you can use larger brushes, but a roller will be quicker and less tiring to use. Good preparation is the secret of all successful painting jobs, so filling and sanding materials are also essential.

PAINTS

Paint works by forming a film on the surface to which it is applied. This film has to do three things: it must hide the surface underneath; it must protect it; and it must stay put. All paint has three main ingredients: pigment, binder and carrier. The pigment gives the film its colour and hiding power. The binder binds the pigment particles together into a continuous film as the paint dries, and also bonds the film to the surface beneath. In traditional paint, this was a natural material, such as linseed oil in oil paints and glue size in distemper (tempera); but modern paints use synthetic resins such as alkyd, acrylic, vinyl and polyurethane. The third ingredient, the carrier, makes the paint flow smoothly as it is applied and evaporates as the paint dries.

The ratio of pigment to binder in a paint affects the finish it has when it dries: the higher the pigment content, the duller the finish. By adjusting this ratio, paint manufacturers can produce paints that dry to a matt (flat) finish; to a silky sheen, eggshell; or to a high gloss. The choice depends on personal preference, tempered by the condition of the surface:

high-gloss finishes highlight any imperfections, while matt finishes tend to disguise them.

PAINT TYPES

The paint types used in the home have different carriers. Water-based paint has the pigment and binder suspended in water as tiny droplets. It is an emulsion, like milk, and is usually called emulsion (latex) paint.

As the water evaporates, the droplets coalesce to form the paint film. Solvent-based alkyd paints have pigment and binder dissolved in a petroleum-based solvent, and take longer to dry than water-based paints. These are known as oil or oil-base paints, although the term "alkyd" is used for some primers of this kind. They give off a characteristic "painty" smell as they dry, which many people find unpleasant and to which some are actually allergic. Because of growing awareness of the health risks of inhaling some solvents, the use of these paints is declining in popularity and is already under legal restriction in some countries.

Paint also contains a range of other additives to improve its performance. The most notable is one that makes the paint thixotropic, or non-drip, allowing more paint to be loaded on to the brush and a thicker paint film to be applied; one coat is often sufficient.

LEFT: Emulsion (latex) paints are available in a tempting array of colours.

PAINT QUALITIES

	BASE	DILUENT	USES	NOTES
Matt emulsion (latex)	water	water, wallpaper paste, acrylic glaze, acrylic varnish; clean with water	basic walls; large choice of colours, flat finish	fast drying, needs varnishing on furniture, marks easily
Silk emulsion (latex)	water	as above	as above; faint sheen	fast drying, more hard-wearing than matt, needs varnishing on furniture
Soft sheen	water	as above	kitchens and bathrooms; mid sheen	fast drying, moisture-resistant, needs varnishing on furniture
Dead flat oil	oil	linseed oil, white spirit (paint thinner), oil glaze, oil varnishes	woodwork; flat/velvet finish	marks easily, not durable
Eggshell	oil	as above	woodwork, furniture; faint sheen	more resistant than above, but still marks
Satin (mid sheen)	oil	as above	woodwork, furniture; mid sheen	durable, washable finish
Gloss	oil	as above	woodwork, exterior furniture; high sheen	tough, hard-wearing finish, washable
Primer	oil	not to be diluted; clean with spirits (alcohol)	bare wood	necessary for porous or wood surfaces
Undercoat	oil	not to be diluted; clean with spirits (alcohol)	between the primer and top coat	saves on top coats, choose the right colour
Masonry	water	not to be diluted; clean with water	exterior masonry	limited colours, apply with a suitable roller
Floor	oil	not to be diluted; clean with spirits (alcohol)	floors, light or industrial use	tough, durable, apply with a roller

HOUSEHOLD PAINTS

These are available in a wide range of finishes, from completely matt through varying sheens to high glosses. There is a wealth of colour choice, and in many do-it-yourself stores you can have an exact colour matched and specially mixed for you. Read the instructions on the can before use to check that it is suitable for your surface. When thinning paint, make sure that you are using the correct diluent.

PAINT SYSTEMS

A single coat of paint is too thin to form a durable paint film. To provide adequate cover and performance, there must be a paint system consisting of several coats. These will depend on the type of paint system that has been chosen, and on the surface being painted.

The first coat is a sealer, which is used where necessary to seal in things such as the natural resin in wood, or to prevent the paint from soaking into a porous surface.

The second is a primer, which provides a good key for the paint film to stick to. On metal surfaces, this also stops the metal corroding or oxidizing. A primer can also act as a sealer.

The third is the undercoat, which builds up the film to form a flexible, non-absorbent base of uniform colour close to that of the fourth and final layer, the top coat. The latter gives the actual finish and colour.

On walls, for which water-based (latex) paint is generally used, the system consists simply of two or three coats of the same paint, unless there is a need for a sealer or primer to cure a fault in the surface, such as dustiness, high alkalinity or excessive porosity. The first coat is a "mist" coat of thinned paint. A primer is also used if walls are being painted with solvent-based (oil) paints.

On woodwork, the first step is to apply a liquid called knotting (shellac) to any knots to prevent resin from bleeding through the paint film. Then comes a wood primer, which may be water-based or solvent-based, followed by an undercoat, then the top coat. To speed up the painting process, paint manufacturers have perfected combined primer/undercoats, and have also introduced so-called self-undercoating gloss paint, which only needs a primer.

On metal, a primer is generally needed. A zinc phosphate primer is used for iron and steel indoors, but outdoors, it is common to apply a rust-inhibiting primer to these materials as soon as they have been stripped back to bare metal and any existing traces of rust removed completely. There are special primers for aluminium. This is then followed by an undercoat and top coat, as for wood. Copper, brass and lead can be painted directly without the need for a primer, as long as they are brought to a bright finish first and are thoroughly degreased with white spirit (paint thinner).

BELOW AND RIGHT: Acrylic primer and knotting (shellac).

BINDERS AND DILUENTS

Pigment needs a binder so that it will adhere to the surface on to which it is painted. As well as the binder in the paint itself, there are other binders that you can add to modify its consistency and texture. Diluents and solvents are added to thin the paint and to delay the drying time. Glazes also delay drying, and modern products such as acrylic glazes can be used instead of traditional scumble glazes for a more workable consistency.

There are many mediums for glazes such as wallpaper paste, linseed oil, PVA (white glue) and dryers that will change the nature of the paint. Solvents such as white spirit (paint thinner) can also be used to clean paintbrushes. Always use a diluent or solvent that is suitable for the type of paint you are using.

Regardless of how you employ them, remember that solvents other than water give off toxic fumes and are highly flammable. Treat them with respect and make sure your work area is well ventilated. Never smoke nearby.

Take care when disposing of empty containers and any rags soaked in paint. The latter can ignite spontaneously if exposed to even gentle heat. Do not pour solvent used for cleaning brushes into a drain; take it to a proper disposal site.

BINDERS AND DILUENTS

	BASE	DILUENT	USES	NOTES
PVA (white glue)	water	water	binder for emulsion (latex) washes	makes the mixture more durable
Linseed oil	oil		medium for powder	lengthy drying
Dryers			add to oil paint to speed drying	
Wallpaper paste	water		dilutes emulsions (latex)	retards the drying a little
Acrylic glaze	water	water	as above	retards drying
Scumble glaze	oil	water	medium to suspend colour pigments	difficult to tint to the right quantity
Methylated spirits (methyl alcohol)	oil	white spirit (paint thinner)	softens dried emulsion (latex)	
White spirit (paint thinner)	oil		paint thinner, brush cleaner	buy in bulk

VARNISHES AND WOOD STAINS

Varnish is basically paint without the pigment. Most contain polyurethane resins and are solvent-based (like oil paint), although water-based acrylic varnishes are becoming more popular for health and environmental reasons, just as solvent-based paints are losing ground to water-based types.

Varnishes are available with a matt (flat), satin (mid sheen)/silk or a high-gloss finish, either clear or with the addition of small amounts of colour. These coloured varnishes are intended to enhance the appearance of the wood, or to give it some extra colour without obliterating the wood grain, as paint would do.

Varnish is its own primer and undercoat, although it is best to thin the first coat with about ten per cent

ABOVE: Varnishes seal and protect the surface of the paint, preserving the finish.

VARNISHES

	BASE	DILUENT	USES	NOTES
Polyurethane/oil-based	oil	white spirit (paint thinner)	strong varnishes in a range of finishes	tough, durable, slow drying
Polyurethane (aerosol)	oil		flat finish	
Acrylic	water	water	range of finishes	not as durable
Acrylic (aerosol)	water		flat finish	
Tinted varnish	oil acrylic	white spirit (paint thinner) water	for bare wood, or antiquing paint; range of colours	slow drying fast drying
Button polish	water	methylated spirit (methyl alcohol)	sealing bare wood	quick drying

white spirit (paint thinner) for solvent-based types, or water for acrylic types, and to apply it with a lint-free cloth rather than a brush so that it can be rubbed well into the wood grain. When this first coat has dried, it is keyed, or roughened, by rubbing very lightly with fine abrasive paper (sandpaper), dusted off, and a second, full-strength coat brushed on. For surfaces likely to receive a lot of wear, it is advisable to key the second coat as before, then apply an additional coat.

WOOD STAINS

Wood stains, unlike paint and varnish, are designed to soak into the wood. Subsequently, they may be sealed with clear varnish to improve the finish and make the surface more durable. They are available in water-based and solvent-based types, in a wide range of colours and wood shades; different colours of the same type can be blended to obtain intermediate shades, and the stain can be thinned with water or white spirit as appropriate to give a paler effect.

Stains are often applied with a brush or a paint pad, but often it is quicker and easier to obtain even coverage by putting them on with a clean lint-free cloth. Quick work is needed to blend wet edges together and avoid overlaps, which will leave darker patches as the stain dries.

ABOVE: Pigments and stains can be stirred into water-based (latex) paint mediums to create unique colours and textures.

A water-based stain will raise fibres on the surface of the wood, which will spoil the evenness of the colour. The solution is to sand the surface smooth first, then moisten it with a wet cloth. This will raise the surface fibres. When the wood is dry, these fibres are sanded off with extra-fine abrasive paper, ready to receive the application of stain.

PREPARATION TOOLS

Two groups of tools are needed, one for preparing the surface and one for applying the paint. For a masonry wall, the minimum preparation is to wash down any previously painted surface. This calls for a bucket, sponges and cloths, strong household detergent or sugar soap (all-purpose cleaner), and rubber gloves to protect the hands.

If the washed-down surface has a high-gloss finish, or feels rough to the touch, use fine abrasive paper (sandpaper) and a sanding block to smooth it down. Wet-and-dry (silicon carbide) paper, used wet, is best for sanding down existing paintwork; rinse off the resulting fine slurry of paint with water. Use ordinary abrasive paper for bare wood.

Defects in the surface need filling. Use a cellulose filler (spackle) for small cracks, chips and other blemishes, and an expanding filler foam, which can be shaped and sanded when hard, for larger defects. To apply filler, use a filling knife (putty knife).

To strip existing paintwork, use either a heat gun – easier to control and much safer to use than a blowtorch – or a chemical paint remover, plus scrapers of various shapes to remove the softened paint. For removing wall coverings before applying a painted wall or ceiling finish, a steam wallpaper stripper will be invaluable.

steam wallpaper stripper

shavehooks (triangular scrapers)

scrapers

sanding block

abrasive paper (sandpaper)

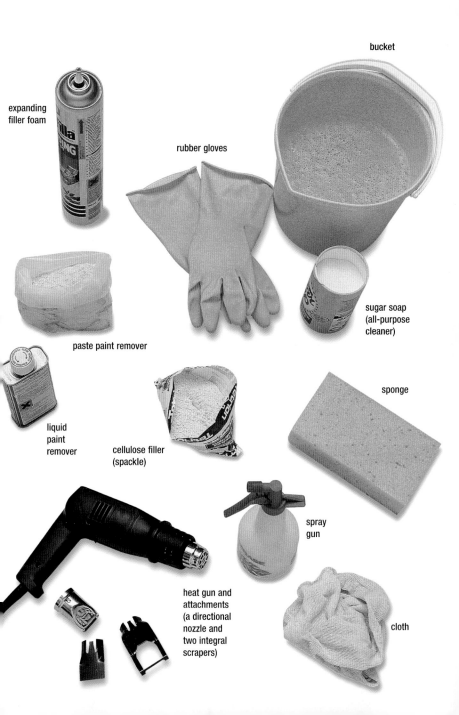

bucket

expanding filler foam

rubber gloves

sugar soap (all-purpose cleaner)

paste paint remover

sponge

liquid paint remover

cellulose filler (spackle)

spray gun

heat gun and attachments (a directional nozzle and two integral scrapers)

cloth

PAINTING TOOLS

The paintbrush is still the favourite tool for applying paint to walls, ceilings, woodwork and metalwork around the house. Most are made with natural bristle, held in a metal ferrule, which is attached to a wooden or plastic handle, but there are also brushes with synthetic, fibre bristles, which sometimes are recommended for applying water-based (latex) paints.

BRUSHES

Brushes come in widths from 12mm (½in) up to 150mm (6in). The smallest sizes are used for fiddly jobs, such as painting glazing bars (muntins), while the widest are ideal for flat wall and ceiling surfaces. However, a wide brush can be tiring to use, especially when applying solvent-based (oil) paints. For the best results, buy good-quality brushes and look after them, rather than buying cheap ones and throwing them away after finishing the job.

ROLLERS

Paint rollers are used mainly for painting walls and ceilings with water-based (latex) paints, although they can be used with solvent-based (oil) types too. They consist of a metal roller cage mounted on a handle, and a hollow sleeve that fits on to the cage and applies the paint. Some can be fitted with an extension pole, which is useful if there are high ceilings or stairwells to paint. Most rollers are 180mm (7in) wide; larger sizes are available, but can be harder to "drive".

There are also slim mini-rollers for painting awkward-to-reach areas, such as walls behind radiators. For any type, a roller tray is used to load paint on to the sleeve. Solid water-based (latex) paint is sold in its own tray.

Sleeves are waterproof tubes with a layer of foam plastic or fabric stuck to

brushes in various sizes

paint-loading container for paint pads

paint pads

masking tape

the outside. Others are covered with natural or synthetic fibre, and have a short, medium or long pile. Choose the pile length to match the surface being painted: short for flat surfaces, medium for those with a slight texture, and long for heavily embossed or sculpted surfaces.

PAINT PADS

Paint pads are squares or rectangles of short-pile cloth stuck to a foam backing and mounted on a plastic or metal handle. The pad is dipped in a shallow tray, or loaded from a special paint container with a roller feed, then drawn across the surface.

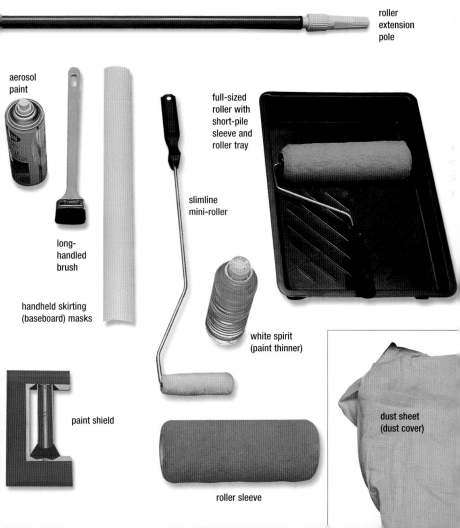

roller extension pole

aerosol paint

full-sized roller with short-pile sleeve and roller tray

slimline mini-roller

long-handled brush

handheld skirting (baseboard) masks

white spirit (paint thinner)

paint shield

dust sheet (dust cover)

roller sleeve

SPECIAL PAINT EFFECTS TOOLS

There is no need to stick to plain colour on painted walls, as there is a wide range of special paint effects that will enliven their looks. The effects here are suitable for decorating large areas quickly and with ease. All can be created with inexpensive tools and materials, and practice and patience will bring highly attractive results.

The special paint techniques consist of very simple effects such as colour-washing and sponging, and the use of broken colour to achieve layered effects with combinations of colour. In using broken colour, a range of different techniques is used to apply a second colour over a different base colour so that the latter still shows through, providing a pleasing two-colour effect.

COLOURWASHING

The technique of colourwashing requires two tools: a large household paintbrush and a synthetic sponge.

SPONGING

All you need for this technique is a sponge dipped into undiluted paint. You can achieve a range of interesting effects by using either a natural sponge or a synthetic sponge. Natural sponges tend to produce smaller, finer marks, while synthetic sponges, such as a car-washing sponge, will make heavier marks.

large paintbrush

colourwashing brush

CLEANING PAINTING EQUIPMENT

Paint is thinned or diluted if necessary with water or white spirit (paint thinner) according to the paint type. Wash tools and equipment in soapy water if using a water-based (latex) paint, and with white spirit or a proprietary brush cleaner for solvent-based (oil) paint. Soak hardened paint in paint remover overnight, then wash out the softened paint with hot soapy water.

natural marine sponge

DRAGGING

For a striped effect, you can use either a special dragging brush, a household paintbrush or even the end of a sponge. The courseness of the tool determines the finished effect.

DRY BRUSHING

A large paintbrush is appropriate for dry brushing.

STIPPLING

This special effect is best achieved using a specialist stippling brush, as it provides a large area of compact bristles. A wallpaper pasting brush or a large household paintbrush can be substituted.

RAGGING

A chamois is used for ragging, but any type of rag or cloth may also be used.

wallpaper pasting brush

stippling brush

small paintbrush

cotton or linen cloth

dragging brush

PREPARATION

Perhaps the most important factor in achieving a successful result when decorating is to make sure that the surfaces are clean and smooth. Careful preparation can seem rather tedious, but it is worth the time spent. Wash walls with a solution of sugar soap (all-purpose cleaner), then rinse them well with clean water. Scrape off any flaking paint and fix any dents and cracks in the plaster with filler (spackle). When the filler has hardened, sand it smooth with fine-grade abrasive paper (sandpaper). Similarly, fix any defects in the woodwork. If knots are showing through the existing paintwork, sand them back to bare wood and apply knotting (shellac). When dry, paint on primer and undercoat to bring the area up to the level of the surrounding paintwork.

PREPARING THE ROOM

Paint is a popular decorative finish for walls and ceilings because it is quick and easy to apply, offers a huge range of colours and is relatively inexpensive compared with rival products, such as wall coverings. It can be used over plain plaster, or applied over embossed relief wall coverings and textured finishes.

Before starting to paint, clear the room and prepare the surfaces. Start by taking down curtains and blinds (drapes and shades). Remove furniture to another room if possible, or group it in the middle of the room and cover it with plastic sheeting. Take down lampshades and pendant light fittings (after turning off the power supply). Unscrew wall-mounted fittings and remove the hardware from doors and windows if they are being repainted at the same time.

Protect surfaces not being repainted, such as wall switches and socket outlets (receptacles), with masking tape. Finally, cover the floor with dust sheets (dust covers), which will absorb paint splashes; vacuum-clean surfaces such as window sills, picture rails and skirtings (baseboards) where dust can settle, and turn off forced-air heating to ensure that dust is not re-circulated into the room.

ACCESS EQUIPMENT

Normally, most of the surfaces to be painted can be reached from a standing or a kneeling position, but for ceilings, the tops of walls and the upper reaches of stairwells, some access equipment is needed. A stepladder, ideally with a top platform big enough to support a paint kettle (paint pot) or roller tray, will be adequate for walls and ceilings.

For stairwells, use steps or ladder sections plus secured scaffold

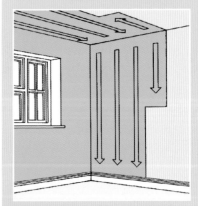

PAINTING WALLS AND CEILINGS

Paint walls and ceilings in a series of overlapping bands. Start painting the ceiling next to the window wall so that reflected light on the wet paint shows whether coverage is even. On walls, right-handed people should work from right to left, and left-handed people from left to right.

boards, or access towers, to set up a platform. Always make sure that you can get to all the surfaces without over-reaching.

PAINT COVERAGE

Paint coverage depends on several factors, including the roughness and porosity of the surface to which it is being applied and the thickness of the coating. For example, the first coat of paint will soak into new plaster, so the coverage will be less than is achieved with subsequent coats. Similarly, a textured surface will hold more paint than a smooth one, again reducing the paint coverage.

Manufacturers usually give an indication of coverage on the container; remember that it is an average figure.

When painting a wall that contains a light switch, protect the faceplate from splashes with masking tape. Paint around the fitting with a small brush before completing the wall with a larger brush or roller. Remove the tape before the paint has dried completely, otherwise the edges may lift as you pull the tape away.

ESTIMATING QUANTITIES

PAINT TYPE	SQ M PER LITRE	SQ FT PER GALLON
Liquid gloss (oil) paint	16	650
Non-drip gloss paint	13	530
Eggshell	12	490
Matt (flat) water-based (latex) paint	15	610
Satin (mid sheen)/silk water-based paint	14	570
Non-drip water-based paint	12	490
Undercoat	11	450
Wood primer	12	490
Metal primer	10	410
Varnish	15–20	610–820

The figures given here are intended as a rough guide only. Always check the manufacturer's coverage figure printed on the container, and use that together with the area to be painted to work out how much paint is required.

PREPARING PAINTED WOODWORK

Modern paints have excellent adhesion and covering power, but to deliver the best performance they must be given a good start by preparing the surface thoroughly.

Wash surfaces that have previously been painted with a solution of strong household detergent or sugar soap (all-purpose cleaner). Rinse them very thoroughly with clean water, and allow them to dry completely before repainting them.

Remove areas of flaking paint with a scraper or filling knife (putty knife), then either touch in the bare area with more paint or fill it flush with the surrounding paint film by using fine filler (spackle). Sand this smooth when it has hardened.

1 Use fine-grade abrasive paper (sandpaper) wrapped around a sanding block to remove "nibs" from the paint surface and to key the paint film ready for repainting.

2 Wash the surface down with detergent or sugar soap (all-purpose cleaner) to remove dirt, grease, finger marks and the dust from sanding it. Rinse with clean water, ensuring that no detergent residue is left, as this will inhibit the new paint film.

3 Use a proprietary tack rag or a clean cloth moistened with white spirit (paint thinner) to remove dust from recessed mouldings and other awkward corners.

STRIPPING WITH HEAT

Every time a surface is repainted, this adds a little more thickness to the paint layer. It does not matter much on wall or ceiling surfaces, but on woodwork (and, to a lesser extent, on metalwork) this build-up of successive layers of paint can eventually lead to the clogging of detail on mouldings. More importantly, moving parts, such as doors and windows, start to bind and catch against their frames. If this happens, it is time to strip off the paint back to bare wood and build up a new paint system from scratch.

It may also be necessary to strip an old paint finish if it is in such poor condition – from physical damage for example – that repainting will no longer cover up the faults adequately.

1 Play the airstream from the heat gun over the surface to soften the paint film. Scrape it off as it bubbles up, and deposit the hot scrapings in an old metal container.

2 Use a shavehook (triangular scraper) instead of a flat scraper to remove the paint from mouldings. Take care not to scorch the wood if it is to be varnished afterwards.

3 Remove any remnants of paint from the wood surface with wire wool (steel wool) soaked in white spirit (paint thinner), working along the direction of the grain rather than across it.

STRIPPING WITH CHEMICALS

As an alternative to stripping paint using a heat gun, you can use a chemical paint remover, which contains either dimethylene chloride or caustic soda. Heat works well on wood, but may scorch the surface and can crack the glass in windows; it is less successful on metal because the material conducts heat away as it is applied. Chemical strippers work well on all surfaces, but need handling with care; for safety, always follow the manufacturer's instructions.

You can choose between liquid and paste-type chemical strippers. The former are better on horizontal surfaces, while the latter are good for intricate mouldings since they take longer to dry. Whichever type you select, neutralize the chemical by washing it off in accordance with the manufacturer's instructions.

Both types of chemical stripper will cause injury if splashed on to bare skin or into the eyes, so be sure to cover up well when using them. Wear old clothes or overalls and vinyl gloves, together with safety spectacles or a similar form of eye shield. Make sure you work in a well-ventilated area and never smoke near the workplace until the stripper has been removed, as the fumes given off can be toxic when inhaled through a cigarette. If you should accidentally splash your skin, wash off the stripper immediately with plenty of cold water.

USING LIQUID REMOVER

1 Wear rubber gloves and old clothing. Decant the liquid into a plastic container or an old can, then brush it on to the surface. Leave it until the paint film bubbles up.

HOMEMADE PASTE REMOVER

Add caustic soda to water until no more will dissolve. Thicken to a paste with oatmeal and use as for proprietary paste remover. Be particularly careful when using this corrosive solution. If it splashes on the skin, rinse at once with plenty of cold water.

2 Use a flat scraper or shavehook (triangular scraper) as appropriate to remove the softened paint. Deposit the scrapings safely in a container.

3 Neutralize the stripper by washing the surface down with water or white spirit (paint thinner), as recommended by the manufacturer. Leave it to dry before repainting.

USING PASTE REMOVER

1 Paste removers are especially good for removing paint from intricate mouldings because they dry very slowly. Apply the paste liberally to the surface.

2 Give the paste plenty of time to work, especially on thick paint layers. Then scrape it off and wash down the surface with plenty of water to neutralize the chemical.

REMOVING TEXTURED FINISHES

Textured finishes are tackled in different ways, depending on their type. Texture paints are basically thick water-based (latex) paints, normally used to create relatively low-relief effects, and can be removed with specially formulated paint removers. Some textured effects formed with a powder or ready-mixed compound are best removed with a steam wallpaper stripper, which softens the compound so that it can be scraped from the wall.

Never attempt to sand off a textured finish. There are two reasons. One is that it will create huge quantities of very fine dust; the other is that older versions of this product contained asbestos fibres as a filler, and any action that might release these into the atmosphere as inhalable dust must be avoided at all costs.

1 Strip texture paint by brushing on a generous coat of a propietary texture paint remover. Stipple it well into the paint and leave it to penetrate.

2 When the paint has softened, scrape it off with a broad-bladed scraper. Wear gloves, and also safety goggles if working on a ceiling.

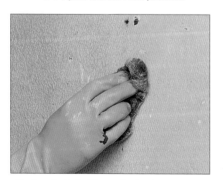

3 Once the bulk of the coating has been removed, use wire wool (steel wool) dipped in the paint remover to strip off any remaining flecks of paint.

4 Remove powder-based and ready-mixed types using a steam stripper, which will soften the finish. Never try to sand off this type of finish.

REMOVING TILES

When faced with a tiled surface, complete removal or a cover-up with plasterboard (gypsum board) are the two options. The former will leave a surface in need of considerable renovation, while the latter will cause a slight loss of space within the room, as well as some complications at door and window openings, where new frames, architraves (trims) and sills may be necessary. In addition, the skirtings (baseboards) will need removing from the walls and refitting to the plasterboard surface.

REMOVING POLYSTYRENE TILES

1 Lever the tiles away from the ceiling with a scraper. If they were fixed with a continuous coat of adhesive, consider covering the tiles with heavy lining paper as a temporary measure. For the best finish, fit a new plasterboard (gypsum board) ceiling, nailing through the tile layer into the ceiling joists.

REMOVING CERAMIC TILES

On a completely tiled wall, use a hammer to crack a tile and create a starting point for the stripping. On partly tiled walls, start at the tile edge. Use a broad bolster (stonecutter's chisel) and a club (spalling) hammer to chip the old tiles off the wall. Have the wall replastered afterwards rather than try to patch up the surface.

2 If the tiles were fixed in place with blobs of adhesive, use a heat gun to soften the old adhesive so it can be removed with a broad-bladed scraper.

STRIPPING WALLPAPER

Once the room is cleared, and dust sheets (dust covers) are spread over the floor and any remaining furniture, the next step is to identify what type of wall covering is to be removed. An ordinary printed paper will absorb water splashed on it immediately; other types will not. To tell washables from vinyls, pick and lift a corner, and try to strip the wall covering dry. The printed plastic layer of a vinyl wall covering will peel off dry, but the surface of a washable paper will not come off in the same way unless it is a duplex paper made in two layers. With paper-backed fabric wall coverings, it is often possible to peel the fabric away from its paper backing; try it before turning to other, more complicated methods of removal.

Printed papers can usually be stripped relatively easily by soaking them with warm water containing a little washing-up liquid or a stripping compound. This will soften the adhesive, allowing the paper to be scraped off. Resoak stubborn areas and take care not to gouge the wall with the scraper.

Washable papers will not allow water to penetrate to the paste behind, so must be scored to break the surface film. Then they can be soaked, but removal will still be difficult; using a steam stripper will speed the process.

Wash all traces of adhesive from the wall and allow to dry before painting.

1 To strip printed wallpaper, wet the surface with a sponge or a garden spray gun. Wait for the water to penetrate, and repeat if necessary.

4 After removing the bulk of the old wallpaper, go back over the wall surface and remove any remaining "nibs" of paper with sponge/spray gun and scraper.

2 Using a stiff wallpaper scraper – not a filling knife (putty knife) – start scraping the old paper from the wall at a seam. Wet it again while working if necessary. Hold the scraper blade flat against the wall to stop it digging in.

3 Turn off the power before stripping around switches and other fittings, then loosen the faceplate screws to strip the wallpaper from behind them.

5 To strip a washable wallpaper, start by scoring the plastic coating with a serrated scraper or toothed roller, then soak and scrape as before.

6 For quicker results, use a steam stripper to remove washable papers. Press the steaming plate to the next area while stripping the area just steamed. Once the wall covering has been removed, wash the wall to remove all traces of adhesive.

FILLING DEFECTS AND CRACKS

A perfectly smooth, flat surface is essential for a good paint finish, and regardless of whether you intend painting a wood or plaster surface, there are likely to be cracks and other minor blemishes that need filling before you can begin painting.

If you have chosen an opaque finish, cracks and small holes in wood can be filled with cellulose filler (spackle). However, if you intend applying a varnish or similar translucent finish, a tinted wood stopper (patcher) would be more appropriate, since it will disguise the damage. Cracks in plaster should be treated with cellulose filler.

Always apply filler so that it is a little proud of the surrounding surface. Then, when it has dried, sand it back to leave a perfectly smooth surface.

FILLING DEFECTS IN WOOD

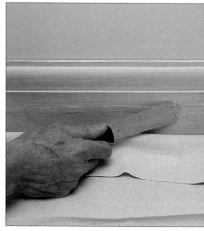

1 Fill splits and dents in wood using filler (spackle) on painted surfaces, and tinted wood stopper (patcher) on new or stripped wood that will be varnished.

2 Use the corner of a filling knife (putty knife), or even a finger, to work the filler into recesses and other awkward-to-reach places. Smooth off excess filler before it dries.

3 When the filler or wood stopper has hardened completely, use abrasive paper (sandpaper) wrapped around a sanding block to sand the repair down flush with the surroundings.

FILLING CRACKS IN PLASTER

1 Use a filling knife (putty knife) to rake out loose material along the crack, and to undercut the edges so that the filler (spackle) grips well.

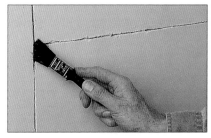

2 Brush out dust and debris from the crack, using an old paintbrush. Alternatively, use the crevice nozzle attachment of a vacuum cleaner.

3 Dampen the surrounding plaster with water from a garden spray gun to prevent it from drying out the filler too quickly and causing it to crack.

4 Mix up some filler on a plasterer's hawk (mortarboard) or a board offcut to a firm consistency. Alternatively, use ready-mixed filler or wallboard compound.

5 Use a filling knife to press the filler well into the crack, drawing the blade across it and then along it. Aim to leave the repair slightly proud.

6 When the filler has hardened, use fine-grade abrasive paper (sandpaper) wrapped around a sanding block to smooth the repair flush with the surrounding wall.

PAINTING TECHNIQUES

The most important requirement for successful results when painting is the proper use of the correct materials and tools. Make sure that you have the right type of brush, sponge, cloth, pad or roller for the specific technique you are planning. Read carefully through the steps to check that you have everything you need before you start.

In particular, make sure that you have enough paint to complete the job; running out could be disastrous. Remember that the quality of the finish will be determined by the effort you put into it. Don't rush or overload brushes in an attempt to speed the work, but bear in mind that you need to keep working from a "wet edge" to prevent seam lines from showing in the finish.

USING A PAINTBRUSH

The paintbrush is the most versatile and, therefore, the most widely used tool for applying paint. Choose the brush size to match the surface being painted. For example, for painting glazing bars (muntins) on windows or narrow mouldings on a door, use a slim brush – or perhaps a cutting-in (sash) brush if painting up to an adjacent unpainted surface, such as glass where a neat edge to the paint film is needed. For expansive, flat areas, select a larger brush for quick coverage. Remember that the largest wall brushes can be tiring to use, especially with solvent-based (oil) paints.

Get rid of any loose bristles in a new brush by flicking it vigorously across the palm of the hand before using it for the first time. Wash previously used brushes that have been stored unwrapped to remove any dust or other debris from the bristles, and leave them to dry out again before applying a solvent-based paint.

Always check that the metal ferrule is securely attached to the brush handle, and hammer in any projecting nails or staples. Check, too, that the ferrule is free from rust, which could discolour the paint. To remove rust, use either wire wool (steel wool) or abrasive paper (sandpaper).

PREPARING THE PAINT

1 Wipe the lid first to remove any dust. Then prise it off with a wide lever, such as the thicker edge of a table knife to avoid damage to the lip.

2 Decant some paint into a clean metal or plastic paint kettle (paint pot), or small bucket. This will be easier to handle than a full container, especially one without a handle.

3 Remove any paint skin from partly used containers. Then strain the paint into the paint kettle through a piece of old stocking or tights (pantyhose), or cheesecloth.

USING A BRUSH

1 To load the brush with paint, dip it into the paint to about a third of the bristle depth. An overloaded brush will cause drips, and paint will run down the brush handle.

2 Tie a length of string or wire across the mouth of the paint kettle (paint pot) between the handle supports, and use it to scrape excess paint from the bristles.

3 Apply the paint to the wood in long, sweeping strokes, brushing the paint out along the grain direction until the brush begins to run dry.

4 Load the brush with more paint and apply it to the next area. Blend the two together with short, light strokes, again along the grain direction.

5 Repeat this process while working across the area, blending the edges of adjacent areas together with light brush strokes to avoid leaving visible joins.

6 At edges and external corners, let the brush run off the edge to prevent a build-up of paint on the corner. Repeat the process for the opposite edge.

USING A PAINT ROLLER

Generally, paint rollers are used to apply water-based (latex) paints to large, flat areas, such as walls and ceilings. Choose a sleeve with a short pile for painting plaster, a medium pile for painting embossed or textured wall coverings and a long pile for deeply sculpted surfaces, such as those created with textured finishes (texture paints). Rollers can also apply solvent-based (oil) paint to flat surfaces, such as flush doors, but tend to leave a distinctive "orange peel" texture rather than the smooth finish left by a paintbrush.

There are some drawbacks with paint rollers: they cannot paint right up to internal corners or wall/ceiling angles, so these need to be painted first with a brush or pad. They can also splash if "driven" too fast, and the sleeves take a lot of time and effort to clean thoroughly, especially if they have been used for a long period and there is dried paint in the pile. Repeated cleaning eventually causes the sleeve to peel from its core.

It is possible to buy a roller washer for removing emulsion (latex) paint. It is designed to stand in a sink and be connected to a tap (faucet). When the tap is turned on, the running water causes the roller to spin and flush the paint from its pile. Oil-based paints should be removed by rolling the sleeve back and forth in white spirit (paint thinner).

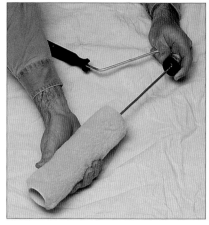

1 Select a sleeve with the required fibre type and pile length, and slide it on to the sprung metal cage until it meets the stop next to the handle. If painting a ceiling, fit an extension to the handle if possible.

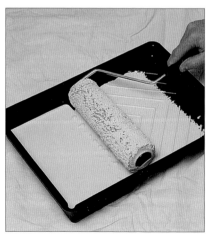

4 Load the roller sleeve with paint by running it down the sloping section into the paint. Then roll it up and down the slope to remove the excess. Make sure the tray is placed out of harm's way so that it cannot be upset accidentally.

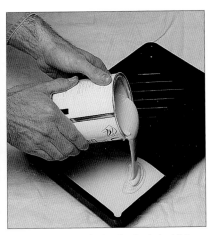

2 Decant some paint (previously strained if from an old can) into the roller tray until the paint level just laps up the sloping section.

3 Brush a band of paint about 50mm (2in) wide into internal corners and wall/ceiling angles, around doors and windows, and above skirtings (baseboards). Brush out the edge of the paint to feather it so that it does not form a seam.

5 Start applying the paint in a series of overlapping diagonal strokes to ensure complete coverage of the surface. Continue until the sleeve runs dry. Do not "drive" the roller too quickly, as it may cause the paint to splash.

6 Reload the sleeve and tackle the next section in the same way. Finish off by blending the areas together, working parallel to corners and edges.

USING A PAINT PAD

People either love or loathe paint pads. They tend to apply less paint per coat than either a brush or a roller, so an additional coat may be needed in some circumstances, but they make it easy to apply paint smoothly and evenly with no risk of brush marks.

For best results, pads should be used with the correct type of paint tray. This incorporates a loading roller that picks up the paint from the reservoir in the tray and applies it evenly to the pad as the latter is drawn across the roller.

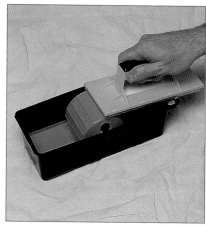

If you do not have the correct tray, a roller tray will suffice. Dip the pad carefully into the paint, then run it over the ridged section of the tray to ensure that the paint is evenly distributed on the pad sole and that the pad is not overloaded.

New pads should be brushed with a clothes brush to remove loose fibres. As with brushes, always select the correct size for the job, using the largest for painting walls and ceilings.

After use, dab the pad on newspaper to remove as much paint as possible. Then wash thoroughly in water, white spirit (paint thinner) or brush cleaner as appropriate. Work the fibres between your fingertips to clean them, finishing off by washing in hot, soapy water.

1 Pour some paint into the special applicator tray. Then load the pad by running it backward and forward over the ridged loading roller.

4 Special edging pads are designed for painting right up to internal angles. They have small wheels that guide the pad along the adjacent surface as you work. Make sure the wheels remain in contact with that surface.

2 On walls, apply the paint in a series of overlapping parallel bands. Make sure the sole of the pad remains flat on the wall. Use a small pad or a special edging pad (see step 4) to paint right up to corners and angles.

3 Use smaller pads for painting narrow areas such as mouldings on doors or glazing bars (muntins) on windows, brushing out the paint along the direction of the grain. The pad will produce neat, straight lines.

5 Some larger pads can be fitted to an extension pole to make it easier to paint ceilings and high walls. Make sure the pad is attached securely.

USING AEROSOL PAINT

Aerosol paints and varnishes are ideal for hard-to-decorate surfaces such as wickerwork. Always follow the maker's instructions when using them.

USING TEXTURE PAINTS

Texture paints are water-based (latex) paints thickened with added fillers. Once the paint has been applied to the decorating surface, a range of three-dimensional effects can be created using various patterning and texturing techniques. These paints are ideal for covering surfaces in poor condition. Most have a natural white finish, but they can be overpainted with ordinary water-based paint for a coloured effect. Avoid using texture paints in kitchens – the textured surface will trap dirt and grease, which is difficult to clean.

1 Start applying the paint to the wall or ceiling surface in a series of overlapping random strokes, recharging the roller or brush at intervals. Do not push the roller too quickly, as it may flick the paint about.

4 Use a texturing comb to create overlapping swirls, working across the area. Practise the effect on paint applied to a piece of heavy cardboard first. When you are happy with your technique, begin on the wall.

5 Twist a sponge before pulling it away from the wall surface to create a series of small, overlapping swirls in the paint finish. Rinse the sponge regularly.

2 When an area of about 1 sq m (11 sq ft) is covered, go over the whole area with a series of parallel roller/brush strokes to create an even surface texture. This can be left for a subtle effect or given a more obvious pattern, as shown here.

3 Give the textured finish the appearance of tree bark by drawing a flat-bladed scraper or similar edged tool over the surface to flatten off the high spots.

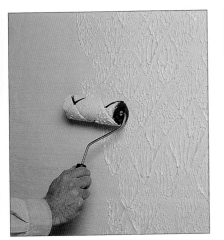

6 You can buy patterning roller sleeves in a range of different designs for use with texture paints. This one creates a regular diamond pattern.

7 This patterning sleeve gives a random streaked effect when rolled down the wall. Apply the texture paint with a brush first if using a patterning sleeve, but do no spread it too thinly, otherwise there will be insufficient to create a pattern.

PAINTING DOORS

The main problem with painting doors – or indeed any woodwork with a large surface area – involves keeping what professional decorators call a "wet edge". Obviously the door has to be painted bit by bit, and if the edge of one area begins to dry before it is joined to the next area, the join (seam) will show when the paint dries completely.

The secret of success is to work in a sequence, as shown in the accompanying drawings of flush and panelled doors, and to complete the job in one continuous operation, working as fast as reasonably possible.

Before starting to paint a door, wedge it open so there is room to walk through the doorway without touching wet paint, and also so that the hinged edge of the door can be reached easily. Remove handles, locks and other fittings; wedge a length of dowel in the latch hole to make a temporary handle for use until the paint has dried. Slide a dust sheet (dust cover) underneath the door to catch any drips. Finally, warn everyone else in the house that

PAINTING FLUSH DOORS

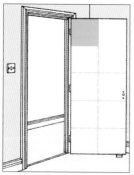

1 Remove the door furniture and wedge open the door. Then divide it into eight or ten imaginary squares, and start painting at the top of the door by filling in the first square. Brush the paint out toward the door edges so it does not build up on the external angles.

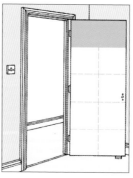

2 Move on to the next block at the top of the door, brushing paint out toward the top and side edges as before. Carefully blend the two areas together with horizontal brush strokes, then with light vertical laying-off strokes.

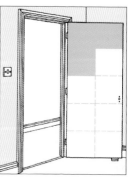

3 Continue to work down the door block by block, blending the wet edges of adjacent blocks as they are painted. Complete a flush door in one session to prevent the joins (seams) between blocks from showing up as hard lines. Replace the door furniture when the paint is dry.

the door is covered with wet paint, and keep children and pets out of the way in another room or out of doors.

If you intend painting the door frame and surrounding architrave (trim) as well as the door, do so after you have painted the door itself and the paint has dried. That way, you will only have one area of wet paint to avoid at a time when passing through the door opening.

PAINTING DOOR EDGES

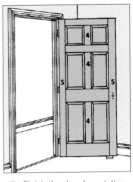

If each side of the door is to be a different colour, match the colour of the hinged edge (1) to that of the closing face of the door – the one facing the room – and the leading edge to the outer face.

PAINTING PANELLED DOORS

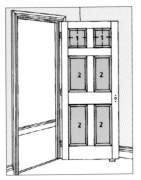

1 Tackle panelled doors by painting the mouldings (1) around the recessed panels first. Take care not to let paint build up in the corners or to stray on to the faces of the cross-rails at this stage. Then paint the recessed panels (2).

2 Next, paint the horizontal cross-rails (3), brushing lightly in toward the painted panel mouldings to leave a sharp paint edge. Feather the paint out thinly where it runs on to the vertical stiles at the ends of the rails.

3 Finish the door by painting the vertical centre rail (4) and the outer stiles (5), again brushing toward the panel mouldings. Where the centre rail abuts the cross-rails, finish with light brush strokes parallel to the cross-rails. Work as quickly as possible.

PAINTING WINDOWS

Windows are more difficult to paint than doors because they contain so many different surfaces, especially small-paned types criss-crossed with slim glazing bars (muntins). There is also the additional problem of paint straying on to the glass. The ideal is a neat paint line that covers the bedding putty and extends on to the glass surface by about 3mm (⅛in) to seal the joint and prevent condensation from running down between putty and glass.

With hinged windows, the edges of the casement or top opening light (transom) should be painted to match the colour used on the inside of the

window. With double-hung sliding sash windows, the top and bottom edges of each sash and the top, bottom and sides of the frame are all painted to match the inner face of the sashes.

Remove the window hardware before you start painting. On casement windows, tap a nail into the bottom edge of the casement and into the lower frame rebate (rabbet), and link them with stiff wire to stop the casement from swinging open or shut while you are working.

PAINTING A CASEMENT WINDOW

1 Remove the window furniture from the opening casement and wedge the window open while you work. Tackle the glazing bars (muntins) and edge mouldings first (1), then the face of the surrounding casement frame (2), and finally the hinged edge of the casement. Paint the remaining top, bottom and opening edges from outside.

2 Move on to paint the glazing bars and edge mouldings (3) of the fixed casement. Use masking tape or a paint shield to ensure neat, straight edges here and on the opening casement; the paint should overlap the glass by about 3mm (⅛in) to ensure a good seal. Paint the face of the surrounding casement frame (4).

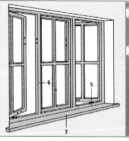

3 Paint the outer frame (5), then the centre frame member between the opening and fixed casements (6). Complete the job by painting the window sill (7) and the rebate (rabbet) into which the opening casement closes.

PAINTING A SASH WINDOW

For best results, sash windows should be removed from their frames before painting. Modern spring-mounted windows are easy to release from their frames. With older cord-operated types, remove the staff beads (window stops) first to free the sashes. Although quite a major task, take the opportunity to renew the sash cords (pulley ropes). This makes it possible to cut the cords to free the window. Some making good and finishing off will have to be done after the window is reassembled.

1 To paint sash windows without removing the sashes, start by raising the bottom sash and lowering the top one. Paint the lower half of the top sash (1), including its bottom edge, and the exposed parting beads (2) and the exposed sides of the frame.

2 When the paint is touch-dry, reverse the sash positions and paint the upper half of the top sash (3), including its top edge, and the exposed and unpainted parting beads and frame sides (4).

3 Finish off by painting the face and edges of the inner sash (5), the staff beads (window stops) and any other trim mouldings around the window (6). Finally, paint the window sill (7). Leave the sashes ajar until the paint has dried to prevent components from sticking.

PAINTING AROUND GLASS

◀ Stick masking tape to the glass with its edge 3mm (⅛in) from the wood. Paint the wood, then remove the tape.
▶ Alternatively, hold a paint shield against the edge of the glazing bar (muntin) or surrounding moulding. Wipe the shield to prevent smears.

VARNISHING WOOD

Varnish is a useful means of providing a protective finish for wood while allowing the pattern of the grain to show through. The more coats of clear varnish applied, the darker the wood will appear, but coloured varnishes are also available that can give the wood the appearance of another species or simply make an attractive finish in their own right. Again, the more that is applied, the darker will be the appearance of the wood, so if possible test coloured varnish on scrap wood first to determine the number of coats you need to obtain the desired finish.

1 On bare wood, use a clean lint-free cloth to wipe the first coat of varnish on to the wood, working along the grain direction. This coat acts as a primer/sealer. Allow the varnish to dry completely.

2 Sand the first coat lightly when dry to remove any "nibs" caused by dust particles settling on the wet varnish, then wipe off the sanding dust.

3 Apply the second and subsequent coats of varnish with a brush, working along the grain and blending together adjacent areas with light brush strokes. Sand each coat, except the last, with very fine abrasive paper (sandpaper).

STAINING WOOD

Wood washing actually stains wood with a colour, so that the beauty of the grain shows through and is enhanced by the colour. The technique can only be used on totally bare, stripped wood once all traces of varnish, wax or previous paint finishes have been removed completely. If they are not, the result will be patchy. Depending on the product used, the surface may or may not need varnishing to seal it, so make sure you read the manufacturer's information on the container. Usually a matt (flat) finish looks appropriate for this technique.

Colours that often work well include yellow ochre, blue, Indian red, violet, cream and pale green.

WOOD WASHES

yellow ochre

blue

Indian red

violet

cream

pale green

1 Pour the pre-mixed wash into a paint kettle (paint pot). Then brush the stain evenly on the wood in the direction of the grain.

2 While the stain is still wet, wipe off the excess with a cloth. This will even the effect and expose slightly more of the grain. Then leave the stain to dry completely before varnishing the wood if required.

SPECIAL PAINT EFFECTS

The techniques demonstrated in this section are traditional paint effects, most of which can be used for all-over impact. They are mainly suitable for decorating large areas quickly and with ease. No special paints are needed, and hardly any special tools, which means that you can experiment with the techniques without having to spend a lot of money. Try them out first on a large sheet of cardboard, hardboard or similar man-made board, changing the colours and adapting the application methods until you are happy that you have found exactly what you need and are confident that you can apply the finish uniformly over a large area. You will be amazed at how attractive these effects are.

COLOURWASHING

Colourwashing is usually done with a broad brush using emulsion (latex) paint diluted with water, wallpaper paste and emulsion glaze to make a mixture known as a wash. The effect varies depending on the consistency of the paint mixture and the method of applying the colour.

In this instance, a large paintbrush has been used, but you could employ a synthetic sponge for a different effect.

Materials

emulsion (latex) paint	paint kettle (paint pot)
wallpaper paste	large paintbrush

COLOUR EFFECTS

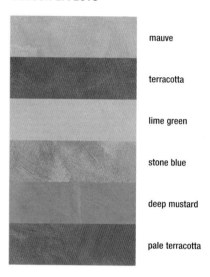

mauve

terracotta

lime green

stone blue

deep mustard

pale terracotta

1 In a paint kettle (paint pot), mix 50 per cent emulsion (latex) paint with 50 per cent wallpaper paste, premixed to a thin solution. Using at least a 100mm (4in) brush, dip the tip into the mixture and wipe off the excess on the side of the kettle. Add the first dashes on to the wall.

2 Without adding more paint, brush out these dashes in random directions, using broad sweeping strokes. Continue along the wall, adding a little more paint as you go and using quite a dry brush to blend the joins (seams).

COLOURWASHING LAYERS

This is done in the same way as colourwashing one layer, but once the first layer is dry, a second colour is applied on top. This layering will soften the overall effect of the brush or sponge marks. Try different colour variations and layering combinations, perhaps using a sponge over brush stokes, or vice versa.

Materials

emulsion (latex) paint
wallpaper paste

paint kettle (paint pot)
large paintbrush

COLOUR EFFECTS

camel under cream

purple under mauve

jade green under pale green

blue under cream

terracotta under yellow

red under pale yellow

1 Mix the paint in a paint kettle (paint pot), using 50 per cent emulsion (latex) paint and 50 per cent wallpaper paste, premixed to a thin solution. Apply with random strokes to the wall, varying the direction as you go. Continue until the whole surface has been covered.

2 When the first layer is completely dry, repeat step 1, using a second colour of paint. Add more paint and soften the joins (seams). The overall colourwash effect will be much softer than when using just one colour.

SPONGING

Sponging is a simple technique that is perfect for the beginner because of the ease and speed with which large areas can be covered. Varied effects can be made by using either a synthetic sponge or a natural sponge. A natural sponge will produce smaller, finer marks, while heavier marks can be created with a synthetic sponge, by pinching out small chunks. You may find edges and corners are a bit tricky with a large sponge, so use a smaller piece of sponge for these.

Materials

emulsion (latex) paint   natural sponge

COLOUR EFFECTS

cream over terracotta

blue over lilac

mustard over white

grey over white

lime green over white

lilac over mauve

1 Dip the sponge into the paint and scrape off the excess, ensuring that there are no blobs left on the sponge. Lightly dab on the paint, alternating the angle of application.

2 Add more paint, continuing to work over the surface. Fill in any gaps and make sure the overall pattern is uniform.

SPONGING LAYERS

The technique is the same as for sponging one layer, but the overall effect is deepened by the addition of one or more other colours. After the first has been applied and allowed to dry, you can proceed with the second, taking care not to put on too much paint, otherwise you will obliterate the colour below. Experiment with different colour combinations, and perhaps try using a natural sponge for one layer and a synthetic sponge for another.

Materials

emulsion (latex) paint   natural sponge
in two colours

COLOUR EFFECTS

orange, red
and yellow

pale green, jade
and grey

turquoise
and lime green

pale terracotta
and yellow

purple
and grey

cornflower blue
and grey

1 Apply a single layer by dipping the sponge into the paint, then scrape off the excess and dab on to the wall for an even pattern. Making the pattern even is not quite so important when applying two colours because the second layer will soften the effect. Allow the surface to dry completely.

2 Wash the sponge out and dry it thoroughly. Dip it into the second colour paint, scraping off the excess as before and dabbing on to the surface. Do not apply too much paint, however, as you must make sure the first colour isn't totally covered.

DRAGGING

A special dragging brush is often used to achieve this effect, but it can also be done with a household paintbrush or even the end of a sponge. The technique is very simple – the brush is pulled down over wet paint in a clean line to produce a striped effect. These lines must be unbroken, so painting a full-height room may prove extremely difficult. To overcome this a horizontal band can be added to break up the height of the room.

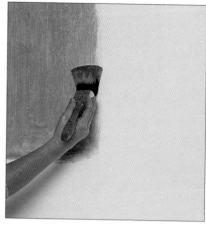

Materials

pencil	paint kettle (paint pot)
ruler	large paintbrush
emulsion (latex) paint	dragging brush
wallpaper paste	damp cloth

1 Draw a baseline. Mix 50 per cent emulsion (latex) paint with 50 per cent wallpaper paste, premixed to a thin solution, in a paint kettle (paint pot) and brush on in a lengthways band, slightly overlapping the baseline. Work on one small section at a time, about 50–25cm (6–10in) wide.

COLOUR EFFECTS

terracotta

brown

stone blue

yellow

biscuit

powder blue

4 Drag straight over the join (seam) and continue dragging in this manner until you have completed the top section.

2 Dampen the dragging brush with the wash before use, as initially it will take off too much paint if used dry. Then take the brush in one hand and flatten the bristles out with your other hand. Pull the brush down with as straight a motion as possible. This will create deep groove lines in the paint mixture.

3 Brush on more paint mixture, joining it up with the last area covered and slightly overlapping it.

5 Once this top section has been done, take a damp cloth and, pulling along the baseline, remove the excess paint.

6 Drag in a horizontal motion across the bottom of the baseline, creating subtle stripes in a different direction.

DRY BRUSHING

This is a technique that uses very little paint. It is similar to colourwashing, but the paint does not cover the surface completely and creates a more textured effect. However, it also emphasizes any imperfections in the surface, so you should consider whether this technique is appropriate before application. To enhance the textured look, make sure that the base coat remains visible underneath.

Materials

large paintbrush   emulsion (latex) paint

COLOUR EFFECTS

biscuit over white

lime green over white

powder blue over white

white over cornflower blue

pale mauve over deep mauve

camel over red

1 Dip the tip of a large household paintbrush into undiluted paint. Scrape off as much as possible and brush on to the wall in varying directions, covering about 0.2 sq m (2 sq ft). Hold the brush almost parallel to the wall and apply little pressure.

2 Continue working in the same way, only adding more paint to the brush when there is hardly any paint left at all. But do ensure that the base coat still appears underneath. Add a little more paint to the surface until the whole effect is evened up and slightly softened.

STIPPLING

Stippling gives a delicate and subtle finish. The technique consists of making fine, pinpoint marks over a wash of emulsion (latex) paint, and it creates a soft, mottled effect. However, it can be quite tiring to do, as the brush has to be dabbed over the surface many times, applying a good amount of even pressure. Two people can speed up the process, one person applying the paint and the other stippling the surface.

Materials

emulsion (latex) paint	large paintbrush
wallpaper paste	stippling brush
paint kettle (paint pot)	

COLOUR EFFECTS

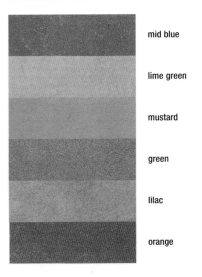

mid blue

lime green

mustard

green

lilac

orange

1 Mix a wash of 50 per cent emulsion (latex) paint and 50 per cent wallpaper paste, premixed to a thin solution, in a paint kettle (paint pot). Brush on a thin, even coat of the mixture, covering an area of about 0.2 sq m (2 sq ft).

2 Take the brush and dab over the surface with the tips of the bristles until the effect is even all over. Continue stippling the surface until there are no obvious joins (seams) and the whole effect looks soft and even.

RAGGING

Ragging can be done in two ways – ragging on and ragging off – and both techniques are as simple as they sound. With ragging on, you dab the rag into the paint, then dab on to the surface. The technique is similar to sponging, but leaves a sharper effect. The choice of colour you rag on over a base coat will dictate the impact of the finished effect. Make sure that the ragging is evenly applied.

Materials

emulsion (latex) paint	roller tray
wallpaper paste	chamois
paint kettle (paint pot)	

RAGGING ON

Ragging off produces a stronger effect, like crumpled fabric. You brush paint on to the surface, then use a rag to remove some of the paint, leaving a ragged print. The recommended "rag" to use is a chamois, as it creates a definite print, although you can use most types of cloth for a particular effect.

When using either of the techniques, it is important to apply the "rag" to the wall with firm, but gentle, pressure. When you remove it, lift it cleanly from the surface without any vertical or sideways movement that might smear the paint and spoil the finished effect. The chamois leather should be squeezed out periodically, as too much paint will result in blobs and drips on the wall.

1 Mix 50 per cent emulsion (latex) paint with 50 per cent wallpaper paste in a paint kettle (paint pot). Pour into a roller tray. Scrunch up a chamois, dip it into the paint and dab off the excess, then dab the "rag" on to the wall.

2 Continue re-scrunching the chamois and dipping it into the paint as before, then dabbing it on to the wall until the surface is covered evenly.

RAGGING OFF

1 Mix 50 per cent emulsion (latex) and 50 per cent wallpaper paste as before. Brush the wash on over a large area.

2 Take a chamois, scrunch it up and dab on to the wall to remove small areas of paint. Vary the angle with each dab. Wring out the chamois when it is a bit too heavy with paint, or the ragging marks look a little too repetitive.

3 Continue working over the surface until the entire effect is even. If you find you are taking off too much paint, apply more immediately with a brush, then dab the chamois over the surface in the same manner as before.

COLOUR EFFECTS

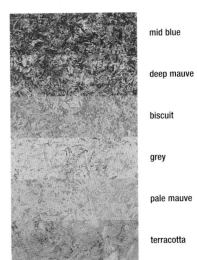

mid blue

deep mauve

biscuit

grey

pale mauve

terracotta

INDEX